What the Things Sang

By the same author:

Objects on Hills
Littoral
Overlay
A Spy in the House of Years
Capital

What the Things Sang

Giles Goodland

Shearsman Books
Exeter

First published in the United Kingdom in 2009 by
Shearsman Books Ltd
58 Velwell Road
Exeter EX4 4LD

www.shearsman.com

ISBN 978-1-84861-054-5

Copyright © Giles Goodland, 2009.

The right of Giles Goodland to be identified as the author
of this work has been asserted by him in accordance with the
Copyrights, Designs and Patents Act of 1988.
All rights reserved.

Cover image by the author.

Acknowledgements
Versions and/or parts of these poems (often in radically
different form) have appeared in
*Oasis, Versal, Shearsman, Terrible Work, Poetry Ireland Review,
Free Verse, Angel Exhaust, Dusie, The Shop,* and *In Fragments,
an Anthology of Fragmentary Writing.*

What the Things Sang

Mojoj dragoj Zori

I am not yet so lost in lexicography, as to forget that words are the daughters of earth, and that things are the sons of heaven.

Dr. Johnson

The map to the finger:
the journey to here starts everywhere.

The phone to the ear:
his name changes radically over the next few minutes.

The spoon to the mouth:
forces we have no contact with determine breakfast.

The glasses to the page:
no one can see the eye evolving.

The window to the curtains:
snowflakes flail down.

The dictionary to the language:
who can number the senses of the word in which I list.

The glove to the key:
my hands are full of blood.

The keyboard to the CPU:
language should be structured like dream.

The glass to the water:
only sand withstands the sea.

The grass to the goat:
you set my panicles trembling.

The tree to the river:
we have rain on our hands.

The river to the fish:
there should be a single planet just for the trees.

The fish to the stone:
a shadow makes itself felt.

The deceased to the boat:
we embarked in careers for the land of the dead.

The water to the cup:
we go so far into a thing and find it has nothing inside but itself.

The eyes to the yes:
the oblivious obvious like the sun we cannot look at.

The pen to the scissors:
reduce poem to newsprint.

The wheel to the road:
he uses his car to sketch an accurate map of the route to work.

The TV to the viewer:
what we have in common with the victim is death.

The viewer to the sofa:
we can use our TV sets to contact the dead.

The corpse to the coffin:
I am a scissors cutting corners across a road-map.

if this—not that
if if is is—then then
if if was is if—now now
if flesh is grass—it sings the wind in the dog-torn field
if the things sing—we would hear rattling inside them
if birds could talk—they would not sing
if the language breaks—there is a word that means both
if objects have thoughts—we would be them
if the trees grit their roots—the peachstone earths you
if you want animals to suffer—teach them to understand
if a shadow never sees the sun—the poem names the shadow
if sentences cannot be finished—we line up our thinking objects
if language is free from its users—it is a god apart from world
if something belongs to your past—it is not yours
if the storming of the winter palace—then the thawing of the spring
if language could explain everything—we would not understand it
if we could understand bird-language—it would no longer be song
if the knife that is each river were to lift—a blade shines in the sun
if time is the rain at the end of the rainbow—it's the wind in the hair

the words are deciding the next
there's nothing less real than its word
nothing changes things like light
a change is a chance gone solid
a tissue of chances makes a person
a person is a mixture of rain
last night's dream is today's rain
we join an association of dreams
shape is the association of memory
mist is the shape of language
mist tries to break through
each word is a potential break
words rust on history's sword
history starts with the full-stop
a full-stop is longer than a sentence
no sentence should be thought
thought is as bodily as taking a shit
a mind is a body of language
the machine in my mouth runs language
a machine sleeps in a closed book
the alarm clock cries itself to sleep
folk-songs are cries of dead labourers
dead objects outnumber the living
flowers believe themselves into life
time flowers on wallpaper
the root of the poem is time
the longest poem is is
nowhere is the capital of nothing
nothing adheres like a road
roads carry blood into the city
a city is as old as its name

desire is a name for forgetfulness
birds convert desire to sound
a bird lands on its shadow
people are shadows that places cast
I do not accept that that
I'll be ready for the end of the sentence
before the sentence language is endless
language connects like a fist
I can connect shadow with shadow
someone keeps watering the shadow
water is superfluous dream
that dream is incorrect
corrections are listed in the hedgerow
the moon shows me a list of the moon
streetlights show through my skin
skin is a readjustment of dust
dust is the secretion of time
time has too many syllables
each syllable says it is a word
words run a ring around trees
a mind rushes like a tree in a breeze
a frame of mind has no window
a window believes in ghosts
there is a belief in the air in the air
at night stars believe in themselves
the night cracks under the door
the door opens under its word
to pass through a door you open a tree
the trees dream shape
a speech shapes the mouth
mouth suggests the sound you make when you make sense
dreams tear on waking at a sound you make
a sense wakens from a dictionary
mountains build into sense without the element of time
a mountain penetrates her eye
the eyes have been to see
a sky questions everything it sees

the dancers' feet are pinned to the sky
leaves dance in the dust of time
the work of the rose fills your limbs with dust
the roses never wake
I am fully awake in the sense mud can be wiped fully clean
you live in the sense
on the skin only bruises are alive
sky is the bruise on the pond's skin
the cloud is making the pond
the moon's wrecking-ball fails to demolish the clouds
the moon bursts on your finger
inside my finger a crowd panics
molecules idle inside a leaf
a leaf comes under a definition
a word struggles to fit its definition
each word you make separates you
sun spreads its syllable through the passages of each city
no plant grows until it is named in sunlight
the plants don't see how loose the stars have been
there are still many stars to flatten into the head
heads are the apples that should not be harvested
the clock tolls in the apple
twice a day the face of a clock shows fear
I write the smile off your face
the best poet writes the worst poems
the poem awaits its driver
harms are waiting in the cloud
a cloud makes itself scarce
judgment keeps repeating itself
the judge is delighted by morning
the morning thinks us out of our sheets
language unites inside one sheet of skin
silence collides with void to form language
shops are empires of void
sand's empire lasts longest
the sand looks past the stars
a sexual object walks past

objects are dissimilar to themselves
a picture destroys itself
you suck in language and exhale pictures
language is the capital of the head
the sky bleeds until there is no capital left
the blood rushes home to be in time for sleep
sometimes things rhyme with their opposites
thought holds no rhyme with word
in your child you hold the limbs of your parents
language's limb climbs across matter
god climbs the wall in the fashion of a flower
the sunset is a flower flowing or a river flowering
at sunset there is fire on the ice
you have been born to be
matter takes form as you
a poem forms the kind of pattern historians dream
we slow down history just so you can listen
I listen to my skin and hear distant birds
a bird lifts the sky with it or from the river
a river seems sincere
a shark seems a shadow
the shadows of god kick among the leaves
god strays between sentences like pollen
a sentence is an insult to name
we are guilty as parents for all they cannot name
the car that contains your parents drives away
beetles mate like crashes depicted by children with toy cars
the child steps into the mirror again
the world of the dead is without mirrors
you commune with souls from the world of the living
death takes souls literally
a cloud takes place
places are shadows that people cast
the daylight casts doubts
you doubt the river in your arms
in the armchair of the cranium sits your fear
my pieces sit together perhaps writing a poem

an artwork sends a piece of mind
through long conduits suffering drains into art
language asks all sufferers to record their impressions
your children are recording you
each child has an inner adult
the sea of the inner eye has no salt
the genital clam of the seabed opens
your wounds open onto the chambers of the dead
the poem shows through in the wound
god does not allow a flawless poem or an unmarked sky
all remarks lead to the sun
when the sun speaks it speaks through us
the kettle speaks its one long word
a word is as long as a line
the regular linebreaks reinforce this reading
a book opens as you read it
each book prints the sorrow of that act
a laugh the shape of a valley imprints on the skull
an apple takes shape and holds
trees take up troublesome positions in the dictionary
poems bleed from dictionaries
the insects write nature poems
the nature of the television washes
each evening we watch the television set
the room pales before the evening
a story is happening in the next room
a story works itself out of some words
the journalist works to fit events into columns
in the event words are broken
a broken moth clings to a belief in light
the moth sleeps inside the mother
Mother Tongue and Father Time blame the children
time grows a beard all over me
the grown man is pulled from you
the man at the end of the scream is hurt
from now your language is scream
as the cymbal sizzles the language is sick

a poem traces a sick god through expression
on waking there is no trace of the war
war extends language by other means
in an ideal language questions would not be possible
a possible god unstiffens in the statue
the statue inside you is stretching
inside the kitten the fire crackles
fire is a word that runs out
these are the words for a song
a song falls into the wrong mouth
mouths are holes in space
the worm finds its hole in you
the train dreams its way through nights to find you
at a station a train stops like history pausing
history starts with the full-stop
there is a full-stop in each eye
the words ache before the eyes   .
we carry before the axe the splinter
the splinter carries the word
the words are deciding.

set the controls for the shape hidden under the dust, the form under the thought, the cold fire of the terminal, the sunbathed rocks, the newsflash, the press release, the sigh of belief, the wedge of light between tall buildings, the war against insight, the space button, the thoughts of the dead, the sides of the coffin, the future poems, the dangerous lives of those inside the television, the felt on the tongue, the content of itself, the cleft left behind when we remove a star from the eyes, the constant inner riot of minds, the defective speech we offer as poetry, the endless corrections we are dotted with, the fists where my fingers had been, the internal combustion of thought, the leaves in a hurry to leave their respective branches, the mothers in whom we were raised and descended, the palette of apples, the particular silence that stars are, the play of words through time, the star tsar, the whites of her yes, the name waiting in the crowd, the blank of an eye, the skin's empty quarter, the grim deleter, the skullcapped mountains, the gravity of the situation, the salt kiss on the chin, the oceanic insides, the first words spitbubbling from his mouth, the kind of life they would once call legendary, the whites at the end of the eyes, the end of the tongue, the minister for the shadow party, the decline of the promised planet, the eclipse first as a fingernail then as a closed bracket, the lichening of stone, the numberless silence of these hills, the skullmasked coot, the statue that a heron forms by standing still, the punctual headlights, the angles we take in order to inform desire, the music they play at the funerals of people you only knew through business, the coded trees, the veinous breasts of Venus, the white goods, the illusion of the illusions of the mass media, the disillusions of poetry, the bland smile of the butter in the fridge, the lives we construct in afterthought, the blank of an eye, the loaded alarm clock, the point of language, the language operator, the unheard poetries, the deadly nightshapes, the kind of smile that could rust a car, the she of wolf, the potentate tomato, the prickly stars, the field infested with cricketers, the mind drained from my blood, the flesh gristled into the mind, the silence of skylines, the moon perplexing the water, the golden potentates, their songs, the smell of destiny and flowers, the degenerative effects of time, the life we are squeezing through, the ragwort star, the dust you requested, the huge sums stored in the notebook of the mathematician, the mighty quim, the lugubrious lungfish, the drunken trees, the blades of glass, the brades of brass, the clouds queuing up to rain on me, the magpie's flypast, the plant revelling under the microscope, the faecal beetle, the caterpillar moving like a severed finger, the ghost from the next world, the last world, the nether world, the h in ghost, the tune to the rest of the song, the shadow of something without substance, the faces that the windscreen-wiper wipes away, the history of seeming, the period of gestation necessary to produce a well formed dream, the sum of the energy your hand had lost, the last train-stop before the journey resumes otherwise, the thumbprint of the photographer in the top left corner of mother's wedding-picture, the scent of miles of fast road, the stain at the bottom of the glass, the dried blood making for the eye, the fragmentation factory, the glass eyes of the television, the slow rhymes the earth makes to keep the language going, the movements of limbs in sleep, the flicker of an eye from word to word, the involuntary body, the bole of a toilet, the ninety six flames that encircled me, the 87 words that make up the foundation of all possible questions, the 82 miles between me and you, the 76 days we accrue on the toilet, the 42 doors out of this world, the 39 situations from which there is no return, the 22 friends I forgot to think of, the 16 pot plants I nurtured, the 5 bricks that start to build the wall, the wall, the words that words want to be made real, the war against insight, the fact that I said this before, the fact, the thoughts that thicken me in the corridor that night, the bone of contentment, the colour of a new emotion that could only be expressed through paint, the figments of other peoples' abandoned novels, the depth of humour, the cloud of knowing too much, the car turning over in sleep, the ghost in the hard drive, the generations each of which took their front pages seriously, the interior ghosts who keep plucking corners of mind, the epiphenomenal residue of sun, the trees riddled with confusion, the rubber perishing on my shoes, the circus of objects, the broken headstone in memory of, the point at which rain ceases to matter, the howl in the lungs of the sea, the song to be addressed to the rest of the world, the sung, the sun.

adjective, correct yourself
animal, celebrate language
artist, return to world
baby, sing the shapes back to sleep
bed, replace the same bodies nightly
bee, be still
bird, alight on your shadow
blackbird, do not forget what you sang this morning
Blake, answer the phone
blink, foreshadow a passenger-jet
blood, play the drumkit in the ear
body, push your arms to the surface of yesterday
bones, place me on the sofa
book, use the library against itself
brain, think of the eye
car, digest in peristalses of traffic
cat, cascade on your shadow
child, leave your heads on the pillow
children, run out of name
city, open like a telephone-directory
clock, turn your hands each way
cloud, get out of my head
commuter, take a train of thought
consciousness, send intelligence across sleep's borders
corpse, sing out of your slit throat
cow, put the blood back in the churn
darling, take the chicken out of the freezer
day, launch your sparrows against me
death, here are the plums I left you
dictionary, define yourself
dog, walk behind your names

dream, worry the children
dusk, crumble the duck before its reflection
eagle, turn to stone
ear, work by bones knocking bones
earthquake, storm the mirrors
ex-lover, call me with a dead telephone
eye, think fast
face, fill space with body
father, open your arm
field, shake off your suit of water
fire, ache for dream
foam, form forth froth
fox, feel under the flesh for the stone
fragment, corrupt the page
friend, part yourself
French people, drink the
geographer, match stone to mountain
ghost, leave the graveyards to mist
glass, scatter light under my eyes
god, enter history
hair, transmit like starlight
hand, speak inside the word
head, contradict nature by thinking
heart, struggle inside your clothes
help, follow harm's way
Heraclitus, sound the absence of thunder
historian, unmake the bed
horizon, climb through the eye
horseman, pass wind
idea, adjust a cloud into a suit of words
if-clause, take things from here
I of the poem, wave hello
immortality, forget us
industrialist, do as the music says
infant, burst the moon with your finger
insect, wing from your name
key, turn the hand

knife, feel the bone
language, name the guiltless
leaves, butterfly beside us
lie, spin your own world
life, dream the inanimate
literature, come apart at the bones
lock, eat the key
machine, run on language
madness, admit yourself
mask, get on with the play
matter, sing us back to sleep
meat, taste mouth
memory, get there before the dust does
meter, make music run for the next line
mind, process the addresses
mirror, part the whole
mist, forget your morning
moon, watermark the page
mother, pass your tongue
narrator, reach in and change the subject
news, tell us the truth
night, report to no one
novelist, struggle to move in your dust
oak, speak swayingly
object, listen to yourself
officer, move the dead on
parent or guardian, tread night's fabric with care
partner, sleep on emotions and wake unconvinced
patient, wake to such things as from a delirium
pebble, make the shadow ground
pen, walk the sentence
pensioner, open the fist to see what the dream
persona, listen to the you of the poem
photo, make your memories come true
poem, write yourself
poet, stop changing your life
poetry, be any text you like

pond, stare the hell out of the sky
presence, feel yourself made
puddle, perplex the world
punctuation, fill the language with dust
rain, shatter the illusions of the pond
river, cut through the neighbourhood like a metaphor
road, run home
sand, drag my feet
sea, run out of words
sentence, scratch the surface of your skin
shadow, meet your maker
shape, hinge a variant world
sir, write the length of days
skeleton, rattle inside the baby
skin, contain yourself
sleep, continue work by other means
sleeper, feel hands grip the sides of your coffin
spectacles, shine unearthly
speech, thumbprint the mountain
spider, exploit the loophole
star, add dark
stars, break your promises
stone, turn to story
story, contain one essential word
stream, wear your name down
sun, drop a handful of change
swift, hold the hidden stairways of air
sword, turn yourself in
syntax, part the words
thing, sing inside
things, hum as if you have mouths
thingsong, sing long
thistle, spike the wind
thunder, guide the poem
time, lift like the tongue of a bell
tongue, work loose
trees, grit your roots

valley, steepen under the feet
watch, feel a shadow on the wrist
waves, remove your tongues
wind, move over us like a good idea
winter, make the coals hot
word, break loose from your sentence
world, let me write you a new kind of song
worm, turn again
year, fall through the calendars

Over the skidmarks of the previous day's pile-up I commute

to the land of the dead until my car runs over the thought-fox

its eyes snarl under tyres a helicopter prints the fingertip of a lower god

pursued by the media giants, their immaterial fists pounding, misunderstood stars

a telecommunications-tower like a cigarette on the horizon, bruises of mid-term sky

swift runs the river down to an organisation amorphous and wavy as sea

not deep enough to reflect so glistening like a night creature that makes scarce

each mist forgets its morning lifting the sun through the rear-view

insinuated into a meadow as clouds add the usual ramifications

thought lagging chemical rashes, washes of light, a police car as a white corpuscle

signals phased so fast you only have time to get in gear before they are red

the roads headlit, in eyelight, then the fields hurt a dissonant yellow, electricity

commuting the rain unmats the fur, a tooth bedded in tar, a crow hops eyes mould into plastic, look again at that field, those leaf-struck trees

the light blank as a computer screen, the corpse by a rush of trembling

the rain in ruins, a familiar crackle, a bluesinger's depth

no field should contain: an uprooted horse, fibrous head, the phone crumbles in

the morning encased with loose threads the foxes and what the foxes eat

print riding over my face and a density of destiny coagulates on the radio

a wheel of seagulls on the field and the road mists up again.

angels impersonate history, animals name god, artists draw swords, atoms celebrate mass, babies construct laughter, beds repeat people, birds make sense, blackbirds particularize territories, blood fills hands, books spread wings, cameras memorize light, cells assemble selves, civilizations produce soil, clauses escape us, clocks ensure midnight, clouds cloud clouds, coins wield pictures, death postpones time, dogs believe us, ducks concern lakes, dust tracks people, eyes seal shadows, fingers control brains, fires bleed consequence, fists empty hands, flowers mark time, fogs ring moons, friends part themselves, god snores us, grass supports flesh, guns fire thoughts, hands shake themselves, history sells books, ink makes concrete, keys turn hands, knives feel bone, language speaks itself, leaves add meaning, light casts doubt, liquids run bodies, locks eat keys, masks leave marks, matter contradicts itself, messages destroy singers, mist rusts swords, money changes hands, mouths catch tongues, myths make sense, names call you, needles sew clouds, nights encrypt us, noun includes verb, paper seals mouths, peachstones earth you, pens draw blood, puddles hold suns, reality bears us, rifles draw soldiers, rivers band together, roads run home, rocks beat scissors, scissors beat paper, senses send sentences, sentences enchain silence, shadows move things, sharks reach conclusion, silence corrodes tongues, skin meets rock, sleep contradicts self, sound comes apart, stars outstare thought, sun forgets earth, thought controls meat, thunder enchains syntax, tongues crush sense, trees bear thought, truth costs lives, tunnels eat cars, voices wear mountains, watches scratch skin, window seals itself, wishes form dew, word is itself.

oil blooms under hills. Birds seep into dark

raining full-stops. We walk through nights

poems are a few years behind the newspapers. To sing in dead languages

time is your pulse. Its glassy face is yours

nights are catching up with you. Imagine your head to be

mud incorporates under the path. These horses in their fields of yellow stars

objects of desire change but not desire. The light turns off not the switch

the trees a day congregates. A few shadows remind me of a few shadows

wind is calling me. A bird lands on its

sing without ever being told we were singing. The sense of a fragile word poised

you commit good acts unconsciously and evil acts consciously. The more aware the worse

under the shores of a house. A mountain wears a cloud

story unfolds like a leaf. The best problems have no solutions

the sentence snarls under the fullstop. Memory, remember me

distort the answer by posing the question. There is a hole in the floor of the sentence

death has the shape of conception's instant. The sperm entombs itself

toes scrape against coke-cans and spears. Here are buried the milk-teeth of previous

but that dream is incorrect. I should have dreamt

another morning. Could this grey really be the most contemporary moment yet

god loves a thought. Each one fills him a little more

dictionary has good definition. To blow-torch the text

puddles have oceans. Shadows have nights

superseding. Footways seed like vestigial parts of consciousness

rather die than be separated from my body. Hitch your wagon to an atom

is the earth we hang from by our feet. The first houses already sketched

in my childhood. I place a finger on the figure I will become

to the specific moment it is not inscribed. O phone explode

a lift rose as the rose lifted. A sink fell as the fall sank

I do not think, think the flowers. The field thinks up the grass

there is enough now to print a planet. It will share most aspects but not be subject to urge

we are the language of instrumentality. The sand made us do it each mouth adds a whole to the language. The moon will hide behind the museum

you find after many years of instrospection your corpse sitting in a rusty car. The engine

a mirror is stronger than a self. A poem is unprotected intercourse

knock through the party-wall to find a family. We do not recognize the faces watching the same TV

at the end of your street a door has your number. You push through and fall

god lifts his face from the mirror. The stars that are his eyes come loose

sounds they made at the dawn of language. Their screams wake us from each skin

later I am driving. I come to a splendid house where

sand is sad. The body of knowledge cannot take a shit

returns time to its notch. The system must end

the subject cancels the future. I is the delete command

worse than entropy is its reverse. No voice dissipating to

it will begin. It ended

addressee, it is important to believe the words are for you
anemone, your sharp stars hurt the eyes
arrow, you are a head of yourself
bishop, the baby opens its wounds to cry
boxer, complex is a word inside a fist
buyer, the cost of consciousness is continual sleep
child, sharpen your days in memory
cloud, you are language
commander, the trains cannot stop
commuter, the road to work is the path home
computer, language unlearns itself in you
comrades, we fabricate each meaning just in time
consumer, the forest closes behind you
corpse, I see your face in the mirror
critic, the text is falling towards you
customer, here is the dark you requested
darling, the curtains are pulling you apart
daughter, laughter is in the shape of a tongue
deceased, your meat is glue
desire, you are unfathomable as the taste of water
diary, the past buried in the rocks is self
dictionary, language is an insult to name
editor, a body of work decomposes here
eye, you move now like a sort of night
fate, you feel what I deserve
fingers, you are numbered
future, fragments of your ash stir
girl, you are the book in the poem
god, the body-mass of insects is greater than ours
hero, your sword is running dry
historian, another moon is crumbling

history, you are a song a labourer forgets
horse, we cannot make you drunk
horseman, your bones are covered in ghost
human, you have a violent bone in your body
husband, time has bearded the children
Klee, your line is waiting
land, there is a civilization consisting of dead people
language, we drive you hard to see where we arrive
listener, the radio is incoherent
literature, thought is replacing you
lord, I shall be in exile in a country I cannot name
love, his clothing is her church
lover, names are to call you
mirror, your vigil never ends
mist, who might speak a name into you
mother, form foams from your forearms
mother-tongue, you involve with questions of roots
mum, your eggs are dying inside us
neighbour, the house is full of broken silence
night, you buckle under media pressure
ocean, every language is in your mouth
page, words scratch you
parents, I came out as other than you intended
path, each decision is where choice flew away
pensioner, the blood is dreaming you out of the door
person, lust is a sketch the body is yet to rise to
philosopher, a poem stands in place of an answer
poem, the language is explaining you
poet, you do not know before you complete the poem
proofreader, in the rough-edits a sentence is like
rain, you disintegrate before our eyes
reader, the leaves of the book of the tree of mind are opening
red biro, you make me feel like my father
rider, your name is written no more
Rimbaud, the drunken boat sinks in the page
river, your name is longer than a tongue
scientist, the atom knows that all words exist

sea, you gather enough silence to build a storm cloud
sentence, you burn at the end of the night
singer, each word is a dead song
sir, the stone birds sing of us
skull, books fold inside you
speaker, the us of the poem moves its lips into us
stone, language is felt on your tongue
sufferer, pain is the only memory of God
sun, you waste no energy
text, here I locate the poem
Thames, run softly or not at all
thing, how you fit the words
thinker, your brain sinks like sand in the hourglass
thought, rain falls like you
time, you renew everything in time
translator, the rain laughs in any language
tree, the leaves are pulling you together
viewer, the news is there to give us the illusion of time
waiter, there's a message in my mouth
walker, wherever your foot is is the path
wife, your fury in childbed is doubled
wind, the newspaper is turning itself
window, sense condenses on the eyes
work, return to normal
world, you become in the guise of flowers or evenings
your honour, we cannot sing through things

if the gurgle in the heating system or the titter of the fridge when you are out were to find tongue

if the tock of the wood as the house shrinks in the cool of evening translated to a message

if as your head rests on the pillow the universal murmur of white noise were to whisper words just to you

if every idea were accompanied by a bing! and a thought-bubble with light bulb that could be read like newsprint

if the sizzle in your pan when you looked down was your own heart

if the rumble of the ringroad were to become tighter every day

if the slam of your door were to sever you forever from what was on the other side

if the static on the radio were to become louder than the music you are trying to tune

if the song at the back of thought were to supersede the message

if the judder of your engine stalling were to bring you to a stop as surely as your heart

if the hums of all the computers were to cease at the same moment

if the trundle of the trolley that brings refreshments at 11.25 each morning were to cease if the boom of all wars were rolled into one that simultaneously deafened killed and enriched

if the clap of thunder were applauding you or if the cough of your engine were to turn to consumption

if the squelch of feet on the pavement stopped at your door

if the whoosh of the toilet brought it all back up

if the throb of a plane overhead were to engorge the sky or if the drone of a missile was programmed to enter your sitting room

if the sum of all the noises were to cancel each other out or if the riff of silence did not break

if the fizz of aspirin failed to reassure or if the tinkle of the spoon dissolved nothing

if the trees were lifting up spokes of thought each of which might be breathed in

if there were a substance that could release you from the hold of the present

if time sends these shocks back then you would stand for a moment in the kitchen or garden or office unable to turn

if when you do turn round everything is the same as it was.

is as if
ice as star
god as verb
work as progress
ideology as perception
a child as a falling giant
the moon as a failed star
the eye as cloud chamber
a rain driven leaf as belief
speech as language of body
language as bodies of speech
the poem as a word for matter
television as the amber of society
the poet as the translator of matter
a poem as an unfinishable sentence
words as the decay the teeth surrounds
the revolution as investment opportunity
sleep as the screen on which oceans project
a child as a form of cancer that grows from us
a person as a dialectic between solid and liquid
global warming as matched by personal cooling
a page contains a poem as a bucket holds sunlight
a leaf falls from a father as a feather balances on the sea
a crowd of people as waiting for the driver inside the poem
the development of writing as mimetic of the development of cities

a two-year-old as perverted by language but reconciled in dreams
a snail as the ghostly embodiment of our ancestors' sexual parts
the way this plant moves as proof of the kind of society I want
self as an island state so small it can fit into a set of clothes
money as what we use when words can get us no further
a poem as a cable for connecting a thought to language
the brain as a surface that has been crumpled inside
the object of desire as the subject of investigation
time as a word so long it contradicts itself
a tree as a book in which all is unwritten
a lexicographer as an organ of the state
the sound of sand as the sand of sound
a poem as an etymology of thinking
a sculpture as anchored to itself
body as the speech of language
skin as too loud an instrument
day as longer than the breath
river as the etymon of road
being as a linguistic object
language as obsolete code
dust as a slow resolution
self as language
star as ice
if as is

how snow falls in the sun

a figure moving in the window across the street

the clouds in your eye

your voice over the phone in early light

your hair reddening at sunset

a child reaching to touch the screen

a child waving minutes after the car left

the red bulb you left me that changes everything

diving-birds moving like planets

chocolate crumbling on the whorls of your finger

the energy of so many roads through the night

the faint firedamp that leads days from now to some quarrel

the compassion of the chemical in the vein

all the needle contains including a decline from godhead

the skidmarks time joyrides over your forehead

the spermy quality of the mist on a March morning

an uncurling of fernheads in the pot

the graininess of the city in evening light

all the colours of the rain

the language the trees speak to each other

the frenzy under a pool's smooth skin

the river-patterns when you close the eyes too hard

sense of obligation to workplace

the lace of friendship that tightens the week

the rhymes nights make in the corners of curtains

the stars that frame this comprehension

the indifferent second that blows world into shape

the pieces of the story that came together years later

arrange these in order of value.

and dissipate into a bath
and procreate universes
and sit in a waterfall at the end of a mountain
and vibrate into the next century
and have someone scratch the exact spot
and stand up suddenly to feel stars
and disturb the air around you
and keep your head six inches from the screen
and be chased madly over the playground
and rewrite the lines of your face
and lift the life from a river
and rotate through the degrees of loving
and let the juice run down your throat
and go out in rain and inhale road
and widen the orifice eagerly
and retain the smell of someone else's body
and lie on your back in a forest
and hold a turd in your mind
and hold a thought in your hand
and nurture inattentive reading
and unhook fragments from sentences
and sleep the moment into form
and light the touchpaper of a beach bud
and fail to hold words
and shrivel the light from trees
and dip your hands in this sentence
and find your fingers abraded
and be contained by the air
and pitch at the sky to see cogs rain down
and feel the planet make furrows through nights
and get there before the dust does
and populate breakfast with sleep's bestiary
and drive slowly, you are driving to work.

The return of the repressed is returning as myth.
The letter before A is the letter God's name begins with

love is the seed stuck in the throat of death.
A leaf is nervous in this light

a war is being fought beneath our feet.
What the forest offers as proof is less than a word

all writing is optimistic: it might be understood.
There is not enough circle to go round

a remark thrown out of a car window is taken up by the wind.
What we think when we think of nothing is nothing

this quality is baked into the product I am naming.
It is not our fault the language is like this

the picture is casting shadows on us.
The I of if is small

where the mind loses, it is often beautiful.
There is money pouring into ideas

sense is the blood fizzing your ears.
The fragment is confused and resting

your hair is like an accumulation of evening.
Each book is a loaded fragment

dance is stance of the distant.
A massive cloud is penetrating her eye

any book is a potential glossary.
The child in this picture is rain

god is drifting between sentences like pollen-grain.
The abyss between sentences is amiss

death is erasing in the trees.
The words repeat and a light glazes the grass

there is no better way home than through your eyes.
What became is what leaves us to become

between the pages is the message we are made from.
Adult self is a planet in orbit around childhood

time is a name the sky files daily in the cabinet marked dead.
Gravel is made of this that scratches the eye

each car is a breath on the motorway.
Death is a waste of dust

a person is the residue of stuff's need to be judged.
The knife is longer than the arm

the best philosopher is thinking in the womb.
The message is lost in the paper

to say is to speak in error.
That is sky or that is memory

the wind is sick but must hurry.
The ocean is too full of tears

etymology is language's subconscious.
There are too many words in the way

a poem is the rust on the sword of history.
The origin of gravity is lost in time

heaven is a face you can no longer name.
The sun is conjecturing people

to write is to interpret capital.
The poem is what should not enter the mass-media

my other body is of water.
As far as I can throw a clock is as long as the moment lasts

memory is an efficient way to dispose of the past.
The body is thick with contradiction

the tongue at the end of the sun is yellow with pollen.
Our sense of illusion is being kept from us

duty is dusty and has many particulars.
It is possible to write this but do not write this

a word is a midsentence crisis.
Milk is your future bones

the brain is a cork to stopper the body's fountains.
A spider is at the end of its ether

a person is slower than a flower.
There is a law or a war against this

the text is falling towards us.
The dark is under attack from more dark

milk is turning in the stomach.
The supply of time is getting harder to maintain

now is always the time to come clean.
A rich source of sound is loose against the tongue

thought is the thread that suspends the sun.
The river is digging its own grave

each dream is an enemy waiting for your love.
Concrete is sand in time's hands

the road is wider than sense.
A book is a tree's foreknowledge

the tongue is the limb of language.
To name a thing is to lie

any book is a potential dictionary.
There is a space built in to days

sex is a scratch on the surface.
A word is bridged by air

the shop is an empty empire.
History is a lie in the armoury of capital

there is no colour in the wall.
Speech is a list of how we know things

a book is spread in its wings.
The indecisions are yet to be made

a river is a string of cloud.
A river is running down its name

property is appalled that the self is not the same.
My current account is governed by tidal flows

the arm of a galaxy is reaching towards us.
Silence's lens is focussing here

there is a murmur where your feet were.
Grass is truth without thought

yours is a colour I hardly interrupt.
My femur is long as your moon

a fire is breaking out under my skin.
There is nothing true the trees do not shake with.

as when a spryng doth fall It tryllyth
as when a bore doth get pigges
as when a mannes stomacke is full and
as when a lion roareth. And
as when a worde doth governe an other
as when a windy tempest bloweth hye
as when a ship An hidden rocke escaped
as when a Gryfon seizes of his pray
as when a swarme of Gnats at euentide
as when a ship flyes faire vnder sail
as when a wherle winde takes the Summer
as when a Nimph Leadeth a daunce
as when a man cannot discerne a dog
as when a wall is broken, and a gate open
as when a thirsty man dreameth
as when a torrent beares blasted Oakes
as when a flash of light Breakes
as when a dwarfe is called a Goliah
as when a Rotten Apple lieth close
as when a tender Rose begins to blow, Yet
as when a hunted Stag, now welnigh tir'd
as when a Chirurgian binds up broken Bone
as when a door in Heaven opened, also
as when a 1000 pound is to be divided
as when a man violently presseth his eye
as when a sovereign queen marrieth
as when a stone lieth still, or a man
as when a Father mourns His Childern
as when a Man hath run fast, or laboured
as when a war is levied, to throw down
as when a Mold repels th' Invading Seas

as when a snake, surpris'd upon the road
as when a torrent rolls with rapid force
as when a Widow comes into Court, and
as when a beauteous Nymph decays We say
as when a dab-chick waddles thro' the cop
as when a Whitlow is upon a Finger, and
as when a child murders his parent? It is
as when a man wills or desires something
as when a stormy gale Roars thro' a hollow
as when a small sum is unjustly taken
as when a permanency is granted him
as when a waveless lake Is sheeted
as when a child cries loud or mournfully
as when a father mourns the dismal end
as when a lover Sees her unfaded cheek
as when a horse tears hay from a stack
as when a man, that sails in a balloon
as when a conflagration has broken out
as when a bird flies low Between the water
as when a musk-scented lady rustles
as when a cannon-ball, missent, becomes
as when a vase of water is jarred
as when a friend reads our verse. Why
as when a sudden spectre at mid-day Meets
as when a thought is swelling in the mind
as when a weir-hatch is drawn, Her tears
as when a man has cancer of his stomach
as when a solid object strikes a hard
as when a city crowds to a review
as when a bar of soft iron is magnetized
as when a leg or a tail is regenerated
as when a dream-figure persists
as when a cheque has been issued but not
as when a body moves in empty space
as when a maggot becomes a fly
as when a large amoeba hunts a small one
as when a train is removed from the timetable

as when a farmer looks down at his feet
as when a historian of ideas is concerned
as when a bird crouches before take off
as when a lot of guests want baths
as when a smudge of ink adheres to a sheet
as when a chief speaks at a council meeting
as when a key nearly won't turn
as when a star becomes protoplanetary
as when a breakpoint has been reached
as when a liquid freezes or comes to
as when a parallel motorway is built
as when a tree dies or is otherwise removed
as when a vocalist's microphone picks up
as when a lewd, diaper-clad infant (played
as when a loose-coupled freight train
as when a hanging drop of water reflects
as when a performance artist uses blood
as when a buyer searches for a seller or

History a gradual erasure of anything that does not make sense

we are angels of history faces pointed into the rear-view mirror

sky: puzzling remains of a history too big to see

rain is the discourse of history

history is a novel that does not have a last page

nothing more passive than history

answer the history according to its process

in the forest a tree's sense of history is persuasive

the world is a sponge for history

outside history there are no moments

history is a secret device for inhabiting clouds

ah sunflowers, weary of history

under pressure of history the stones band together

freedom: the length of the rope that connects us to the end of history

in the history of meaning there is one slot open

sitting in a bath with a toddler is part of history

how people dream will be the same history that poems construct.

or seize the sea inside the moment
or suffer sleep's instrumentality
or wait for each dream in turn to come untrue
or show the moment the door
or try every sentence as closure
or write a book in which no adjectives are correct
or read Heidegger only as you imagine him
or assemble an album of anthems of defunct countries
or turn the idea against yourself
or walk the grey line between chaos and ice
or hold each word down until meaning comes out
or concentrate night into the knots of stars
or look through the smear
or unpeel the labels from night
or stack the shiny empty cans of thought
or accumulate verbs like money
or erode the tongue
or jerk the moon from its socket
or hook down some stars
or dream about being dreamt about
or inhale the worlds of a crowded room
or have a quickly repressed violent or sexual fantasy
or dream the telecommunications giants
or argue with your shadow
or let the hours show their wounds
or live in a house made of thought
or struggle against an immovable abstraction
or share a hotel room with the time
or stub your head on a pillow

or release words from definition
or combine thought with oxygen to act
or consist of too many dimensions
or perceive as tree
or rub night between a hand
or compose yourself into fragments
or make a list of everything you have forgotten
or say nothing. Say it till you're hoarse

each word is a hinge to a parallel world, it is as long as a line

every night you produce a double, in a weakened state you blink away you

everything is in alphabetical order, in between scattered a few dream-sequences

every object and action is given a Dewey number, even thoughts

the sun has been exploding for so long, it looks normal

the past is like the future, unlike the future

night explains in writing so dense, it eludes everyone

knowledge can be suspended in consciousness, not dissolved

your food has been consuming you, your buildings building you

nothing can be measured, although structures still hold up and no catastrophe occurs

Moses bears the first tablets of concrete poetry, but society is not ready to understand

recollection enumerates skin, and when I scratch planets scale away

advertising occupies the place of art, and the only lines are engraved by the sea everything answers to its need, to think of a desire issues its fulfilment

people travel in time at different speeds, you only know those who share your velocity

we are composed of time and silence, or some mixture of sand and effort

time flows back or forwards at any moment, and we reflect on each action *sub specie eternitatis*

robots are run-of-the-mill, and every teenager can transform into a daemon from another dimension

it's only electric charge that keeps us from falling through floors, like a book is mostly paper but only words

the traffic of knowledge takes on forms never seen on the earth, blossoming in electronic night

we have forgotten how to go home, and ride our horses over uncharted pasture

extra dimensions have been tucked away, or the distinction between bosons and fermions does not hold

there's no more fun to be had and no more victims, learning and science prevail

clouds whisper endorsements, satellites are arranged in corporate-identity constellations

god human animal and plant are at one with each other, Siva the creator-destroyer sits in a lotus

arbitrary distinctions have been obliterated, and national identities are multiple and polycentric

earth is the shadow of heaven, chaos and cosmos are superimposed

there is an aphrodisiac for every emotion, and a cupboard in which to store how we feel

walking back from the car dreams ask us what is inside the rain, and what inside the thing inside that

at the end of the nerves there is a person who with grace receives all messages, and like a great necromancer tells the present

the usual ways of looking dissolve, and people stir with green desire

it is permissible to pursue one's end without regard, and other people are worth what they believe themselves to be

a leaf has fallen from the calendar, but time is still.

are there realizations waiting
are these birds aching for us
are we moments of light

can a thing be full of its possibility
can I have the same state of mind twice
can the point of entering work be identical to the week or year before

corpse, do you speak

do all words turn against themselves
do you speak language

does a smoke of feeling blow out as you sit to the end
does joy produce somewhere else a corresponding pain
does the feeling that I am lessen the knowledge that you are
does the past outweigh the future
does the present tense defeat you
does the world change for you

if the answer to everything were discovered what would change
if you mean hard enough will you be true

is it size that makes us small
is there a time when all cycles will have run

shall road always postdate path?

you arrive somewhere else by following the same road to and from work
you remember the smell of a road from childhood which has no name
you will be waiting, your mood depending on much I can't explain
you are being massaged by an assortment of demons and sprites
you are afraid to open your eyes in case the world rushes in
you have so little to say that only poems are quiet enough
you play in the fields where time for the first time moves
you can't see why one second is different from another
you are displeased by the sound of your own laugh
you are as positioned in history as the next chapter
you do not come to the door in case it is yourself
you would have to screw down heaven to fit hell
you are being billed for consumption of daylight
you speak to me on the other side of the page
you have to understand the dream repeatedly
you are ready to move to the next paragraph
you are too nervous to enter your clothes
you are strong or strung enough to leave
you are as far as your eyes cannot reach
you are a stain on the book of history
you fall from a book like a black petal
you wear out an atlas in search of me
you are being discharged into the air
you can hear the sun call your name
you are incapable of finishing a day
you are in range now. Don't move

a torch with no batteries sheds enough light to see the unconscious

after my thoughts have made love to each other sometimes there will be a poem

all roads lead to Rome but all footpaths process you back to your mother's house

children play in some fields then roll them up and take them home

clouds connect as consecutive dreams in all shades of rain

concentrating under soil may be a new anxiety waiting to happen

corridors of hospitals in which we were allegedly born shine with alien light

dark amounts to storage of information around the sleeping form

days fall open to reveal an underside in which we or the weather yolks out

death touches you like an old lover still familiar with your skin

each moment a new self falls leaving your body a cemetery for millions

Father Time and Mother Tongue are collecting their children

fields are graveyards from which we pull skeletons of wheat

horses in their fields decide not to be

however many newspapers you read you will not come across these

ignorance grows until when you reach old age you're stupid

in the underworld they speak the language of dead flowers

language musters together some people so that it can be talked

lies add up to a composite picture of something true

mind recurs over a fragment of language that will not fit

mistakes are written in the name of language

most dreams are forgotten because most are untranslatable

my children have not come home because they have not been born

nights shift the boundaries between one house and another

often I correspond with the moment gathered around me

our shape is conical with an egg at one end and a corpse at the other

silence is as long as creation but there is always the numbering of stars

sky is a documentary about cloud shapes on the biggest screen yet

slow noises break no windows but the speed of thought outpaces planets

spaces between lies and the patterns they make are as close as we get to truth

the gentle way this plant moves is proof of the kind of society I want

then he says something untranslatable

there are languages where other suns leak through

to touch the brain is to provoke unseen fragments into tearing through me

trees seek the kind of clarity that comes through rubbing against air

under the Japanese faring of a grasshopper the engine runs cold

unexplained nations rise from advertisements in magazines

we are necessary to triangulate the stars

words tangle with sense to produce a problem or a poem

world presents as a series of windows to which we give the names of days

you've come in through the front door but the house is wrong

your thoughts are in a pattern you do not see until the end.

if a person sets enough words a book threads the eye

if the eye contains a river the tongue feels its silence

if silence is bone as the page ends so does the mind

if mind is a wording of form the clouds inside the hill make sense

if senses are left by planes flowers open their faces to speak

if flowers are going home possibilities burn under wheels

if I wheel home light echoes from the sun

if the sun is a sheet of paper under the door letters seal the dark

if in the dark potatoes put out legs night progresses like a story

if the story speaks it never learnt to whisper

if parasites whisper in the ear they control dreams

if my dreams are banal I go back to sleep

if snow sleeps under the door I oil locks in the prisons of language

if a body of language is a book thoughts are too fragile for words

if words are in the wrong order we join them with things they never make happen if you happen to see through the tired eyes of history wake up

if a wind wakes some embers they get up and open history

if history could speak its apology would be inaudible

if apology spreads through streets the TV is the eye of other worlds

if a world leans against an eye a language is about to fall

if we fall towards language when we land it's time to wake

if time's surface stretches we sleep in the curves it makes

if a snake fucks itself to sleep the hill sharpens like flint

if only hills are older than rivers choice clouds the sky

if rain falls from a clear sky a horse stands under its own steam

if a horse rests its bones settle into soil

if soil sweetens under bone the unconscious of nature is manufactured

if there's a stream of consciousness it's a roadful of noise

if the hinges where road meets path open all the doors jam

if you scrape the door open you understand the shape of hills

if hills are blunted the trees build smoke out of self

if selves are guilty there's no trance like every day

if the sun spends the day on a *roman fleuve* the moon rewrites history

if the moon sulks into the night she wants to say so much

if the truest thing we ever said was our birth-cry we forget why

if we forget how to move our limbs sleep is unanswerable

if sleep amounts to a sheet of paper it builds into a seam

if you finger the seam in a doll's thigh memory is a production of time

if texts travel through time you are only here in person

if you are not the person who fell asleep find where you put your face

if I climbed through my face I'd name the silence

if silence rephrases itself the trees speak in shadow

if the shadow of a tree boils on the lawn the paper is made of cloud

if clouds accumulate like a bad mood the moon doesn't blink

if a thin-lipped moon denies everything I agree with most of what I am

if I contain meat the weight of tongue is terrible

if my tongue speaks it says it is in fact nothing

if dad's nothing more than a mountain of bones I'm still climbing him

if he climbs himself there follows a passage of voices

if words won't voice each other we walk through equivalence

if you walk from one side to the other of yourself you must be god

if god is a child she never gets bored of the lightswitch

if all of the facts have come to light light has burnt them away if you burn your shadow on the drive history lacks a last page

if the printer dreams of a page a house is a tray of people

if you open people words spill the text of that moment

if a text dissolves in contrail dreams are up in the air

if a war is fought in dreams there is no trace when we wake

if regret wakes in corners of mind the sky will find the right colour

if a willow swings against sky it arranges itself in order of seeing

if the things could see beside these hills fold the arms of beside

if the car disintegrates before my arms I'm not the way you imagine

if the meat imagines us it is a story howled in darkness

if a story is as long as we are it grows cold

if thought grows words the only word I'll write will be the word word.

envision the shrapnel of an exploding universe
a totalising consciousness encountering its reflection
the wind inside the grid of each day
new perspectives on domestic appliances
the edge of a time before edges
chlorophyll concentrations on the planet
the sun obscured by gunsmoke
the moon's nightside illuminated by earthshine
a butterfly sucking tears from the eye of a buffalo
a black chiffon tube dress patterned with gold spots
winglets and tip bulges developed during research
a trefoil of parachutes lowering the used rockets
neuroblastomas invading the spine of a 6-month old
an action figure with his own TV series
the fountains we never waded in
the arrow at the centre of the road
the light from a torch when the battery is low
the adolescent years looping inside
a film in which I thought I was the central character
a convolution in the brain of an ant
the feeling objects we sometimes hold
the road that snakes to itself
the congealing of stone at oceanic depth
my children lining up to fight me
the moon through a thousand litres of fog
forgetful water streaming where we last put the clouds
the nervous trees of spring
the lichening of stone
the leaves that the tree photocopies
a world coated in different languages

how can we distinguish thought from space
how could we run out of things to name
how deep is an eye
how do the clouds see us
how do we fit the events of sleep into hours
how do you entertain a thought
how long is your head
how many die as the result of inaction
how many maps make a tree
how many times does history repeat
how many whispers make a shout
how many words express a moment
how much does the twentieth century cost
how much do words weigh

in what sense can you say that is true
in what sense is a field undermined by words
in which sense of is is this

is it I or the night that is cold

on whose decay is your destiny built

to whom does this corpse belong

what are the chances of being born
what aspect of self is coming to light
what colour is living brain
what consumes days
what divides the light between cities
what do things sing for
what do we keep as dark as the brain
what else happens in the dream
what gathers these as my thoughts
what if the sum of knowledge does not add up
what if what haunts me is self
what is destroyed by language

what is the air holding back
what is the it that is inside this
what is the sense sensing
what is the song singing
what is the sound of a street with no traffic
what is too solid to name
what kind of poem is world
what lies behind air
what purpose holds in the clouds
what saddens the lute
what is it that the clocks are adjusting
what is rain a metaphor for
what will the watch not count
what wipes the wind's fingerprints
what works under the words
what would we see if money quit its work of representation

when shall the dead outnumber the living

where do we store lived experience
where do words sleep when we do not release them
where does light come from in dreams
where is the shine inside darkness
where would you put the sky
where would you start a history of reflection

which is true: light or shade

who can't feel ash shelving at the bottom of the shoe
who coined the sun
who is at the end of the shadow
who is watching through my eyes
who ploughs the clouds
who sets the flowers, their fire
who wound the dead?

by screaming inside
by default of imagination
as deep as the dark
as their major shareholders
by pretending the alarm is not set
by telling it stories
as long as the story you are
as many as were born from action
as many as the map depicts
as many as will return us to the garden
the number in the head
this many
it cost the lives of our parents
it weighs according to the gravity of the sentence

in the sense carried in the word
in the sense that is imputed to it
it is the is inside the will

it is I and the night that is cold

on the decay of those on whom you stand

to the owner belongs the corpse

unbelievably remote and inevitable
the aspect of the open fist
the colour of the dying skin
the people driving their selves home
the consciousness of time
they sing for an undivided self
we keep nothing so dark
my feet stick to the train
the great fists of cloud
we will be the remainder
I jump out of his skin
everything it names

it is the it that is inside it
the mockery of the animals
that nothing and air are too solid to name
an unrhyming limerick of considerable length
the sound of heavy plant breathing
it is the tongue at the back of the head
it is the phone at the sound of the air
a different category of air
the end of the above
a door that opens in the grass
the words that cannot sing
a thing that cannot be felt
watches do not count
the lake at sunset, the eye
the paper, the scree, the pixel
the eyes of a child with the eyes

they did so from the start

it cannot be stored
in beds of paper, in trays of sand
it is generated by dark
everywhere you look
out of the door, out of the eye
it must start with the surfaces of water

neither one nor both

those who are ash
it was forged, not coined
the idea at the end of the theory
the person at the end of the nerves
the dead folksingers of any nation
the flowers do it themselves
the dead wound the living but the living cannot wound the dead.

nothing recedes, there is only capital and the weather, against each other

the kingfisher, an affront to concrete, waits as the sky rolls away its blueprint

poem-fragments fall into the page as the sun, like a brilliant practitioner of the eye's holes, slides down a cast bronze sea

time, by which means we recall lost sentences, is narrated by the sun

the sun, necessary so we don't see stars fucking, closes us

history, the loops of a signature in which are ideograms for each repercussion, seals no documents

our children, messages we can't finish, look for punctuation

arriving at work, as if at a destination, the screen fills like a pool

you look down at your wrist, scarred from your watch, to see that you are a field

we settle into cars, without the capacity to dream, and drive towards sleep

except we are also the food, we are laid out like it was time to start eating, and feel hunger

a blackbird, singly, transmits a scrupulous unscrewing of the moon

tonight, the car alarms are calm, a puddle on the path is a window to a different world

those thoughts, watch out, or they will never be recovered

driven by sleep, clouds stagnate the stars, the traffic accelerates the evening's dream

you contain many rivers, not all of them named, and one ocean

there is a train, bearing your name, waiting at a station

the history of forgetting, including a footnote on how things stand at this instant, closes

there are cities under the roots and mullions of earth, still to be opened, and you

after my thoughts have made love to each other, sometimes, there may be a poem

language, if it could speak, would be silent

time sounds like this, the severed tongue is severe, language is the first casualty

here, as if language clumps and thickens, the words undo

as I have had occasion to note previously, my ears sing, my throat aches

capital, in using language, is vulnerable to interpretation

grandfather, shouting across a century, is indistinct

if there was only one star, mighty and knowing, it alone would know us as we really feel

wandering the earth, the traffic comes to a place it has not heard before, it stops and reports

How it was a mistake. I meant to say

how fine these trees are
on the horizon, defined by cloud,
but what I said was

how a blackbird conjugates a song,
but what I wrote came out

how those full-lipped tulips sneer at me
witheringly from the wastepaper bin
but it became measurable as

how this image passes through what the head
insists is the mind's eye
but I could not get beyond

how this tremble under the tongue signifies
speaking, the sigh that hung in the air
that was really a comment on

how I had often been struck before by

how to convey the experience

how what connects and what makes real
are different signs for what lasts longer,
me or the breath in me were

how to find a way to recall
the objects stored inside the skin,
but here was only

how the dog ran across the field
like the shadow of a dog
the speaking clock spoke, it said

how this will reduce down to
the memory of a single word
from which the meaning has been lost

how like the forgotten words of a song,
or the hum we used to fill the blanks.

what it is and what it is made of
here now and here then
a canned show and a live event
a person's net worth at the start and end of a year
a political decision and a lifestyle choice
a child and a dwarf
a clang and a clank
a blah production and wow work
qualities in bodies and ideas attached to them
a standard model and a $500 upgrade
a fake and a repro
how it is and how it should be
a mitral murmur and a bronchitic rale
a solar day and a tide day
an animal and an automatic statue
a state of nature and a state of grace
the song and the words
inactivity and inertness
actual and expected costs
confused and faint vision
the routes of planes and thoughts
the pattern in the clouds and in the ocean
an engine building itself in the sun and a plant
a slit and a slot
the shape a thing is and the space it takes
what's said and what's intended
considering a motion and performing it
the disturbance and the words
a map of everything and a map of nothing.

it is as if   I am listening to a distant   but enthralling storyteller   turning the page   or briefly clearing her throat. It is as if the centuries hushed their wings and waited   it is as if till this strange year of dread and wonder   never one rosebud blew.   It is as if for thee the very march of thunder   halted, and lightning's red lips silent grew.   It is as if the flowers in prehistoric valleys   had waited for thy reign.   It is as if I   had thoughts like a girl   blushing in the branches. It is as if there were being woven a cloth shirt made of the fibers of   dead men, and of course it will be perfect. It is as if a drum were beaten in the streets   far from my island, and I heard an ocean hammering a shore. It is as if the whole marvel of the world   had blankly died,   exposed, inert as a drowned body left   by the ebb of the tide. It is as if they heard under the grass,   the dead men of the Marne, and their thin voice   used those young lips to sing it from their graves,   it is as if the warm sunlight   in some deep glen should lingering stay   when clouds of tempest and of night   had wrapped the parent orb away   it is as if the glassy brook   should image still its willows fair   though years ago the woodman's stroke   laid low in dust their gleaming hair: it is as if we were each   a painting and hung on some   gallery wall   and now the painting turns   upon its back. It is as if the siren understood   how that she is so strong at this still hour, that I could not repulse her if I would. It is as if a corpse had power to feel   the tying of its hands. It is as if you're lying in a field of rye, In ringing blueness, falling heat it is as if angels were waiting to up-hold him, if it came about that he leaped from the height. It is as if the book opens, showing the parts you have played   in a theatre more precious to you than the Globe   it is as if Night itself   meant to cherish me it is as if the youthful green   that drew us as lovers together   were no more than a gathering   sheath, a knot of meaning   the reader was eager to find. It is as if the garden were   always there, even where we are,   here, where war is,   the certain   end, the paradise. It is as if the muted air   were made of the down of their wings   of the sound the hushed sound   of their wings which none but another bird could hear.   It is as if the first light were made for singing   it is as if Dante were walking   from roof to roof   lightly singing   a muted melody. But it is as if I were waiting for him to start,   as though he alone had the key to that door   it is as if He has located Himself inside a theatre of His own design and choosing. It is as if the universe turned back,   (the greatest poet, in fact the only one). It is as if Helen wanted to recall her immediate 'family', as protection or balance against the overwhelming fact of her Fate or Destiny. It is as if some eons-old mind (in a time when it could do those things) cast the future on its cold eye, saw Plato's cave, and became our brains. It is as if you yourself were your own onlooker. Simultaneously from all sides, bird's-eye view it settles within its metallic sheen. It is as if the tenderness   had been distilled for other purposes, leaving a residue of sludge. It is as if, without knowing it, we all   suddenly longed to be diminished it is as if Life his Sister, as if the Blessed Virgin, (his own flesh, his own sister), as if Nature made wise by God's Art and Incarnation were to stand over him. It is as if someone had slipped   a double-edged knife between my ribs   and hit the spot exactly. It is as if   my father could speak   His huge body   silent and massive   and under the cold white skin   solid shit. It is as if you have entered Into a lion's mouth. The smell of Jeyes and the smell of dung rise to the roof it is as if my heart   put on a face and walked into the world it is as if I listened To the philosopher of a strange sect   describing his homeland. It is as if a whole warehouse of books lies under water, the books stacked on their sides; the pages congeal together in pure amnesia it is as if nothing happened   though those who lived it thought that everything was happening it is as if, by shouldering them, feeding statements to the monster,   she might distract it into letting her off. It is as if I had become somebody else   not by becoming another person but by becoming   some of the things one person may seem to another. It is as if the Sarmatian horsemen came back,   Yet they do not stir, or make themselves visible. It is as if nothing in the world existed except metaphors. Or as if all our words without the things above them were meaningless. It is as if somehow the lovers of postage stamps had created an image of themselves. A red wheelbarrow or a blue image of the unknown. It is as if they or you observed one continual moment of surf breaking against the rocks. A textbook of poetry is created to explain. It is as if there exists a large beach with no one on it. It is as if we were never children. Sit in the room. It is true in the moonlight   that it is as if we had never been young. It is as if   Men turning into things, as comedy, stood, dressed in antic symbols. It is as if   We had come to an end of the imagination,   inanimate in an inert savoir. It is as if in a human dignity   two parallels become one, a perspective. It is as if being was to be observed,   As if, among the possible purposes   of what one sees, the purpose that comes first, the surface, is the purpose to be seen. It is as if life were stretched upon a rod and   we no choice to make but spare the self, lord, from   falling off that high wire it is as if   a sweet-scented flower   were poised   and for me did open.   and for me did open.

No road is as long as a dream or as short as a memory

news has a concession-stand in the pavilion of dreams

the reason we don't remember most dreams is most are untranslatable

meaning is just the surface of the dream

the medium of the dream is time

we recount dreams in the present because we can't leave them

raise up each dream against capital

we are dreamed by the edge of thought

sometimes I can dream up to about one star in Halliwell

a closed book recounts the dream of a windblown tree

we have to pay for dream-crimes in daylight

when I cycle to work everything else follows as a recurrent dream

flawed lives are perfected in dreams but perfect lives are subject to flaw

poetry forms the kind of pattern historians dream about

how come these dreams hold in place

we accrue through life a charge of dream

within the context of the dream I am pleased with this thought.

Abandon your clothes and swim on, accumulate night's matter behind your eyes, address your fingers towards me, adjust your dust, admire mist and turn from its edge, alchemize night into poetry, alphabetize your thoughts, argue shares into values, arrange the lines in order of value, assist the child who is struggling in to her new robes, awaken the statue inside you, be true to the words you have been exercising, believe the broken mirror, break into your constituents, brush light from trees, build a second of silence, burn away the masks and the marks they leave, burst the moon into the reverse of song, call it a cloud, catch a complicated sentence in midair, chant the things into their places, clang time against the doors of midnight, clank behind you your chains, close like a flower, collapse the world in the eye, come to the moment as a hunter comes to the prey, commit crimes to see if your body will fit them, complicate the act of reading, compose letters to the sun till the clouds come home, conceal the head in which grubs pulse, connect tongue to cloud, consume time, contradict what the words told you, count the eggs perishing inside, cover the skin with reason, crack like a joke, cross borders including these of language, cross-refer to a poem in which there was a different character saying this, define it by dreaming, derange the orange and the water whispering in the drain, descend into a new poem, destroy words to find that each one is a buried sentence, disinter winter's innards, dislike poetry, distil ink into blood, distort the answer by posing the question, distribute smiles until each taker goes away empty-handed, divide the wind into thinner layers, do not adjust your sex, draw a map of the sky now to guide you on your journey next week, dream a satisfactory work environment, dress in time for your name, drop words into the dream, edge the silence with bones, embark in careers for the land of the dead, embed in the leaves these voices, ember the nights we had, enter a land where travel is destination, erase the last poem, erode the myth under the stylus, err on the side of excess, estrange the poem, exchange all things for fire, exhume the buried popes line them up and then tell them the truth, expand an idea to fit the right cloud, explain how a Jesus Christ lizard walks on water, fear what language might say, feast on a rare word dug from its paper, feed the hungry monuments with drafts of blood, fight silently against your newspaper, fill things with what they are, find the word to fit the song, fix to its muscles one person against that self behind, follow the chains of causation to reach the last answer, form forth from foam froth, frame this in a pair of glasses, free the dinosaurs from their stones, gather notes towards a poem you already wrote, get vertigo from the strata of a diary, gloss words until they shine, glue events together, grind the sky into particles of light, harm your vocabulary, historicize the elements back into their sleeps, hit hard the space button, hitch your car to each atom, hold a thought in your hand, ice the crimescene that will be your skin, imagine the blood of those you consume to be the liqueur in chocolates, increase night's value as you store it, inflect harm on those you sing for, influence history by speaking out of place, institutionalize the means of thought, invent a new cancer which becomes fashionable in certain areas, launch at the face of the spectator the spectre, lay a finger on the figure you become, learn from stones to stop falling, leave disturbances in language, let be be still, lever open the paint-pot of dawn, lie back and let sleep think for you, listen to the voicemail that tells you that there are no messages, live lives each night and on opening your eyes forget almost everything, locate the voice in the poem, look before you read, love make, make so bold, melt a poem into the civilian population, memorize the wrong way home, mistake yourself for a person who bears your name, nurture children by ignoring them, obey language, oil the buried machine, open a bracket, outlive the masks of nature, part the words to see inside, particularize always, pass an echo down the corridor, peel off and blow away the synonyms, pick up the floor from the floor, picture the exhaustive light, play the larynx's syntaxes on thought's saxophone, portray more deities in our sitcoms, praise the buildings for standing up, print the memorials of today on yesterday's lawns, privatise the dead, proffer space and let time do the taking, pursue an image to its conclusion, put what the sun can't say into likeness, reach for the sensing stones, reassure the night hanging from the tree and the children wondering from their beds, recollect the broken headstone that says "In Memory Of—", reduce poem to newsprint, reflect blood from puddles, release the imprisoned poem, relive the dead in song, remember your mother printing her lips on you, remove the sword from the sunset, reopen the dead tenderly, replace words with their partners, resolve light into its constituent shadows, retract the sky and peel off the moon, return each leaf to its tree, rhyme with word, ride the nonstop trains of consequence, rotate the sounds until they fit their names, scatter the sentences to the page, scratch the surface of nothing, seal the child in the word, see poetry as the best history we make for the robots, seek each jewel of rain, sever world from its dream about itself, shake loose nights like dust from a rug, shelter from the news, shut your mouth and pour out darkness, sing the wrong words out of the song, skip to the end of the line, sleep through what the day explains itself to be, sound like absence of thunder, speak thousands of languages all of them English, spell the night into a word, spend your life, split open a hoover-bag and pull out long forms of dust, stalk the hollows where your cheeks form, start building the planet under our feet, stir a poem out of embers of moths, stop saying anything that contains its own words, stroke the back of your thoughts, suck in language to exhale image, take me to the cemetery which contains James Joyce, tend the map, tender the hands to ash, throw your arms in the air, transmit the matter-torn spirit to the bird outside the air, trap a rare word in a poem, travel through nights and glimpse the new newspaper, tremble the light into its shape, turn art into fragment, underthrow the government, undo the package the light came in, unfasten the puddles, unlearn your operating languages, unrot the flowers, unsocket this moon, untie bridges like strings, use the language of advertising against production, vary the world, wait for a moment that justifies everything not knowing you are waiting, wake screaming into a new set of clothes, walk into the mountain at the end of the list of mountains, watch for the suppositional madness of these too-distant-to-see birds, weigh the evidence, work out in any world where the door is and lock it, wound open your song, write what you do not already know.

we are in a sea of sound that laps us **&** we swim in music
we swim in music **&** each song has its glossary
each song has its glossary **&** all flags are the same
all flags are the same **&** nothing makes anything
nothing makes anything **&** poetry makes poets happen
poetry makes poets happen **&** lines float down
lines float down **&** time sometimes deepens
time sometimes deepens **&** the river runs more slowly
the river runs more slowly **&** the car hits morning with a snarl
the car hits morning with a snarl **&** the streetlights turn off in front
the streetlights turn off in front **&** the sky fills with language
the sky fills with language **&** each tree is a wholly owned subsidiary
each tree is a wholly owned subsidiary **&** you are travelling through light
you are travelling through night **&** silence is a balance of opposed forces
silence is a balance of opposed forces **&** I'm an impression the air gets
I'm an impression the air gets **&** a house swallows me sometimes
a house swallows me sometimes **&** each human shoulders the next
each human shoulders the next **&** we come to the gate marked world
we come to the gate marked world **&** you lose your weight in skin-cells
you lose your weight in skin-cells **&** you are mostly dust
you are mostly dust **&** you surf channels
you surf channels **&** mountains pull inside
mountains pull inside **&** you are contained by the air outside
you are contained by the air outside **&** night is engraved in the eyelid
night is engraved in the eyelid **&** days are painted on the eyeball
days are painted on the eyeball **&** there should be a chronology of space
there should be a chronology of space **&** there must be a map of time
there must be a map of time **&** dreams require no proof
dreams require no proof **&** a person operates as a universe
a person operates as a universe **&** the space between thought is infinite
the space between thought is infinite **&** the shape of shapes is indeterminate

the shape of shapes is indeterminate **&** space has no enemies
space has no enemies **&** lines of force never intersect
lines of force never intersect **&** what cannot be repeated is true
what cannot be repeated is true **&** you're momentarily aware of a secret task
you're momentarily aware of a secret task **&** the dead are happy in silence
the dead are happy in silence **&** there is illumination in decay
there is illumination in decay **&** seconds end with a whoom of blood
seconds end with a whoom of blood **&** I move as much as the sea
I move as much as the sea **&** what I say solidifies
what I say solidifies **&** you feel time's heat on the hand
you feel time's heat on the hand **&** there's a sound for each feeling
there's a sound for each feeling **&** these sounds are not words
these sounds are not words **&** to sigh is to sing in snake language
to sigh is to sing in snake language **&** to sniff is to whistle in dog-talk
to sniff is to whistle in dog-talk **&** silence dissolves into earth
silence dissolves into earth **&** clouds are the thoughts of hills
clouds are the thoughts of hills **&** you are earthed to peaches on their trees
you are earthed to peaches on their trees **&** one bite roots you to stone
one bite roots you to stone **&** many doors to burst through
many doors to burst through **&** when I push them sleep spills from my eyes
when I push them sleep spills from my eyes **&** nothing makes anything.

the lost languages each of which has a word for

the emptiness of playgrounds during and just after rain

the quality of an alarm clock before it rings

the smell of apples on grass

the emotional state of a word

the lost empires packed into history

the sound a word makes when left alone

the collected weight of past selves

the capacity of abstract statements to draw a concrete response

the story from the aboriginal point of view

the accumulation of books over a lifetime

the gigantic involutions of the intestines

the transports waiting in seconds

the bad side of good actions

the different doors you came through to get here

the amount of space you fill in one in-breath

the link between your mind and cancer

the last forest you walked through

the way what you saw gets mixed with what you saw on TV

the art of remembering differently

a hairline across a field

the forgetting inside the clock

the wind in the window

the rain in the rainbow

the sea inside the moment

the smell of a wet god emerging from behind the arras

a world that still contains us but only just

a full mind on an empty stomach

someone shouting SILENCE

the silence before a word like thunder

the trail of decay that leads back to your front door

hotel rooms through which people recur

the numberless silence of these hills

the statue a heron forms by standing still

this journey as long as language

the awkward gesture the light makes at this time

the pattern too many silences make together.

I	a small title in another person's library
in	the way out
this	a meaning which cannot name itself in language
self	a multiple occupant of the same shell over time
rain	the content of itself
time	woven into your clothes but you cannot trace it to meet your skin
sleep	spending some small time without illusion
brain	a limb that can grab a galaxy and particularize the mote
death	an accumulation of fullstops
a river	a machine for parting light from reflection
a poem	a mirror being broken
history	the softening of pears in a bowl
mistrust	made of mist and rust
a desert	a coat of sand
language	the machine that made us
the word	as close as we get to the god
the event	in the event
a hoverfly	a single bead on an invisible abacus
happiness	an effect of serotonin
a sentence	at least two illusions having a fight
perception	relative to ice melting on mountains
philosophy	using last week's TV guide to tell you what's on tonight
an explorer	following the map that shows how to lead the life of an explorer
a pine cone	a slow hand grenade
mass media	without mass
in the event	the event
nevertheless	nevermore
a blade of grass	a feat of arms
winter's interior	cupped in a tree
sky's reply to earth	moderated by earth's knowledge of ocean
night's equilibrium	maintained through the cries of animals
travel through time	funded by everyone's willing belief
the ignorance of bliss	so profound we can't tell who woke the neighbours
the indifferent second	blowing world into shape
the thought of hardness	a substance to push
the mouth in language's flesh	too fragile to name

In a world in which smoke sank, we are unaware of a fire's beauty.

In a world in which communication is bodily, blind people invent speech.

In a world in which continental drift happens fast, weather forecasters say what coastline you'll be on.

In a world in which selves peel off after each transforming experience, people avoid art.

In a world in which babies speak, they tell of life on different worlds.

In a world in which death takes the place of love, telephones connect people randomly.

In a world in which narrative is compulsory, lives begin upon a time and end ever after.

In a world in which Darwin is misguided, scientists describe small gods evolving into species of moth.

In a world in which there is no present tense, yesterday and tomorrow were simultaneous.

In a world in which the celestial company occupies the entire space, there is no room for reflection.

In a world in which freedom is total, we lose the use of our limbs.

In a world in which each person is an actor, there are no curtains.

In a world in which souls of the dead gather, the conversation is short of laughs.

In a world in which we live in a state of truce, we lose sight of peace.

In a world in which all facts are true, they still contradict each other.

In a world in which time is food, the fattest is fastest.

In a world in which everything happens, it happens slowly.

In a world in which to make a child you make love thousands of times, the love determines the child.

In a world in which poems are machines for relaying thoughts, they become you briefly.

In a world in which hills slant the words that the wind lost, we cannot catch them.

In a world in which massy thoughts build up, arteries of the brain haemorrhage.

In a world in which the continents send messages to each other, they can't be spoken.

In a world in which thunder undoes the clouds, matter is translated through music.

In a world in which silence rusts, the statues walk home.

In a world in which sculptures regard us, we create a machine that will laugh back.

In a world in which things happen in newspaper-size blocks, journalists come with glue and paste them down.

In a world in which there are as many histories as voices, some are louder than others.

In a world in which time stands on its head, days spill out like lost toys.

In a world in which the forest burns when we look into it, opened books think us.

In a world in which sleep is shadow, we never see it until our light is turned off.

In a world in which the tongue has no language, it speaks for everything.

In a world in which we are nature's chance to see itself, *I* occurs to you now.

In a world in which history doesn't unfold any more, it unreals.

In a world in which to open a door is to close one, a room is a feeling you do not enter.

In a world in which be is a transitive verb, I can am someone.

In a world in which all the poetry has been written, it will be time for the world to end.

In a world in which I must live, I invent differences.

god *as* just one of my several million names
eyes *as* windows for matter to see itself
time *as* a particle of awareness we crash into continuously
wind *as* the thoughts of trees
sleep *as* the synthesis of night and consciousness
nature *as* a composite of algorithms
matter *as* a stable form of energy
history *as* a nature made up of texts
comets *as* comments on passages of history
a poem *as* an unfinishable sentence
the slug *as* graffiti artist
the U. S. *as* a 3,000-mile broad comic-strip
memory *as* shining a torch in a cathedral
rainbow *as* a fabrication of sky
the body *as* composed of memory
the songs *as* thinking through us
the world *as* a representation of divine nature
the dream *as* artform
the mouth *as* an exit wound
our bodies *as* the recording instruments of deities
each nostril *as* the concave opposite of a hand
a work of art *as* never complete until it is unfinished
people on TV *as* exiles from the real
aphids on a leaf *as* cattle in a field
a segment of space *as* inside each eye
the crown of a water-drop *as* a symbol of eternity

the years of being yourself *as* an aggregate
the answerphone message *as* from myself
the miles that separate us *as* air
being away from home *as* being closer to truth
the electric field *as* a swarm of photons
a field of wheat *as* a skeleton army
your mouth *as* the tongue's home
Plato's cave *as* the retina
the tongue *as* connected to the feet
pregnancy *as* proof of other dimensions.
the dream *as* trying to understand you
the womb *as* a gateway from other worlds
any poem *as* an act of opportunism in the face of silence
starlight *as* a carbon used too many times
a mirror *as* a machine for capturing souls
thought *as* weak electric charge
the sun *as* the remote control that switches us on
a poem *as* a way to make language look silly
history *as* an untitled poem
gravity *as* matter's love for form
poems *as* epiphenomena of statement
cancer *as* a light in the eye or a tiny branch in the ear
unjust *as* an antonym of adjust
leaves *as* the sense-organs of trees
rivers *as* the remains of rain
poem *as* a machine made of worlds
body *as* a flock of related neuronal acts
sleep *as* the water of the evolutionary past
time *as* a compendium of information
dust *as* still searching for home

The last word is the first victim.
The first in line is the last time.

The lord of the dance is the prince of darkness.
The storming of the Winter Palace is the evening news.

The god of small things is the devil in the detail.
The top of the morning is the bottom of the barrel.

The old man and the sea is the dead rising.
The heart of darkness is a light skin.

The start of something beautiful is the end of the affair.
The mist of time is the fog of war.

The invisible man is manifest destiny.
The wild swans at Coole are flights of fancy.

God's gift to women is the eternal feminine.
The call of the wild is the cry of the loon.

A handful of dust is a fistful of dollars.
The worm in the bud is the fruit of our labours.

The land of the free is death's dream kingdom.
The narrow road to the deep north is the M1.

The proof of the pudding is one man's meat.
The fly on the wall is the pattern in the carpet.

The ghost in the machine is the genie out of the bottle.
The decline of the west is the triumph of the will.

The ascent of man is the scent of a woman.
The woman on the verge is the foolish virgin.

A crumb of comfort is the best thing since sliced bread.
The men they couldn't hang are the babes in the wood.

The rust in the joints is the iron in the soul.
The white of the eye is the light at the end of the tunnel.

The ship of fools is the barge of state.
A labour of love is the play of light.

The way of all flesh is the corridors of power.
The beast with two backs is what no man can put asunder.

The rock of ages is the sand of time.
The grapes of wrath are the fruit of crime.

The man with no name is the Unknown Soldier.
The tree of knowledge is the root of the matter.

The road less travelled is the path most taken.
The man who wrote on water is not forgotten.

The republic of letters is the realm of the senses.
The last judgement is the first prize.

Self eludes me like a word someone says in sleep as the night is quiet
then a thought sails away trailing its feelings in the sea's abstraction
as I wake and the plovers in the field in the valley explain why the
notes are twisted as I'm a small rectangular hill pulsing dawn but I
have the account which makes me individual as much as the face I'm
trapped behind consequently I slip into consciousness as I put on the
same shirt I've worn for years when the finger is beside the point as
the song dies in the throat if in a dark room a word is as nothing to a
match in consequence its decline became visible as soon as language is
written in some sense this which for the tongue is time ticks as word
afterwards death's limbs tremble for me as moths prepare to invade the
autumn vegetables up till now something has shifted a continent away
as the pinlit inlets of your face are ghost despite which we spill out
like words so come to a planet marked exit as it will be time to begin
otherwise lichen draws a map around us as the wing of a plane falls
secondly what history unfolds to us is as unstable as a poem where
the river in the dark is humming water's unceasing syllable as each
star is surrounded by its shadow where I confuse a fly for the cursor
as I can't see why it's moving over the screen yet we are left alone
in the forest as the moon bumbles through the clouds of us unless
the days come down like dark birds and perch where we should live
as the children are recording us whence the message recounts the
imponderable nature of sex as people crowd into themselves from
the dismembered hills skin flashes into this that names itself as a desk
waits and beside it some pot plants so that ghosts deploy speechless
ambassadors as the song sinks in the soil or most daylight squashes
into reflection as it requires the muscles of a hundred thoughts to
counter each advert in which case time fastens you in the persistence
of mist as the ghost in the dictionary spirits world into word as if to
say various errors are being keyed as the sense ends at the stalk of the

eye in other words the trees print a list of birds as the sky files them
daily into the cabinet marked dead from the moment folk-memory
constructs from media images as the mighty rose lifts and says 'the
phone cracks as waves splash light at me before the poems of the dead
radiate from their earths as a cloud hails unless a tear stands for an
emotion and falls as water particularly the tongue is a key sticking in
the mouth as the particles slake my hands or shake inside hence leave
the weather out in the weather as shadows climb over themselves
moreover a package of years falls by the wayside as the souls are
driving and in addition I forget what the idea is I translate in my head
as the road strikes me as textual in nature or to put this otherwise a
leaf falls from the nineteenth century as it lands I read it in order to
consume my weight in packaging as the fruit rots into me whenever
I drive to the burial ground under the supermarket car-park the
silence falls to pieces at my throat as the ice globs downriver thirdly
consciousness hangs in low air as I hear the distant birds weeping
over their lost meanings consequently I taste the air and seize the
slightest route as possibilities chain themselves to my clothes while
in some languages the word for moon changes monthly as the old
word picks up and flies on to find new senses if the sky rings like a
drum as the animals fall particularly my feet describe a circle as the
earth quicks however a child hits a space button as sand flows into
my veins up till now mothers surround me raising their arms as the
machine guns open' at this point my feet loosen and the skin listens
greedily as the shadow spools from a pen when in the shape of the
valley on the back of a skull I return to such lost spaces as days edge
off the maps now we build our white interiors like cloud as we invent
one sentence unless night is a narrative murmured as pages riffle with
the voice of the wind despite which the body embraces decay in
sleep as a possibility leans open on the other hand I make no mistake
as consciously as retreating into sleep before there is nothing in this
except night advancing as it has always done actually stars function
in a way similar to advertisements as a figure walks across my eyes at
a time when the sun sandcastles among hills as we come to the same

conclusion as night consequently evening remembers hazily the tricks of morning as night returns as an emotion while the curators set in to catalogue the dust as the museum decays or in a town like this people don't often wake in the small hours as one word is being spoken by a child but the sky hides behind a sheet as the prisoner whistles a few bars out of the window and walks free.

'I' is a poem that writes itself in action or in inaction and sometimes in language and somewhere past the window drips the dawn or everything will be mentioned in the end yet light cracks the shell of night or the skeleton in the crisp-packet but it hurts in almost every direction or there are records buried in my clothes so the page is trembling or travelling under the lamp after there is a story happening in the next room concerned a child getting into his body or trying to catch it as it grows away from him because I'm waiting for my child to be born or to collect him from the cinema although sitting through another film as the light sickens slicks form underfoot or underarm whenever his eyes clog and he laughs off his shirt or stands like a lamb in a pure theory of language since the child is man to the father or teaches him the growth-value of bonds so that his clothes are collecting him or time disinclines him as if there is nothing left but rocks or between the rocks algebra whether everything deserves to be seen unclothed or the ghost retires from another breathing match while children are the enacting of sunlight or a bird has the ephemeral answer in its beak nonetheless when I breathe bits of me enter the world or I'm the thing in the air otherwise the meat tastes in the mouth or the house we are in is our father similarly I ask questions of ancestors and they say things like 'it is time now to cross those bridges that hold underneath a small portion of light or taking your children home from their labours remember to remind them what they owe you then nobody is an advance on nothing or the television

is the terrorist indeed the tree is made of bones or the letters of the
songs in the book's boarded mansions meanwhile there is a drunk in
the forest or the forest is drunk perhaps a spider shatters a pond or
suddenly is now if I were to write a visual poem it would look like
this   or perhaps this provided I lie in place waiting for the meanings
or their many and different clothes since each trip costs too much or
the voice is probably only the kind of cough that kicks away the props
night stands on then three wise men make a vow or the devil speaks
in prayer yet I am not a being or I am a becoming whether she comes
inside still wearing the rain or the senses are being to see unless we
are upstream from death but paddling hard' or a dream opens where
the grave yonders though the hooded kettle breathes heavily or the
messenger stays his tongue hence the particles of me are snowing
or we make strange together albeit I consume my weight in air or
float up and see how work left its marks on me again since those the
language names are guilty or dark sings where you cannot listen but
concerning that which we know there is little left or it will all come
untrue assuming that a colossus collapses in a light wind or dream
creatures invade the living and there is a name waiting in the crowd or
the night crumbles before thinking.

The person the shadow touches turns to me because I is a mother
or my clothes are struggling with me because it is hard inside yet the
children are tired before they are born because they have to think
when the hedges write a pitiless poem in berries because the rain
in the trees is waiting or the days coagulate from nowhere this thick
jellyish light I'm obliged to walk through because anything else is
wrong so I sense sometimes what the clouds have been building
because it is a function of the air but knowledge furs in the brain's
kettle because water is hard however we weep behind the car and
drive because people have heads they use to locate themselves with
when they awaken even so God places me in the document because
I'm an angel in relation to what existed before and each question
is eventually answered by the weather because forms spend years
practicing shapes such as 'tree rock cloud' and you in fact the birds
are laughing in code because we are language also in the musculature

of a spider there is no room for expression because tongues do not work in their mouths therefore your eyes are glasses containing the time before clouds because objects like the way they feel after all by walking we connect with nothing because when the trees answer there will be no ears subsequently the shadow bursts into a room and holds in its hand an idea that must be written down quietly because the message is shhhh inasmuch as the words are broken keys because the language fits similarly a judgement is continuously being made in my absence because I have to reject so many doors in order to walk home although for years I stumble home to the wrong address and no one tells me because the clocks are not sure unless I've heard the mermaids arriving by car because their laughs tinkle like glass on the drive for instance words stay still because they are useless namely we dig back in time to build chalk soliloquies because by the railroad we made strange provided that a different if is here because all around us cry those long dead rumours of air whether or not it takes years for a soul to ascend even a small distance into the atmosphere because downdrafts spin them back to the earth nevertheless we fall apart at the clothes because night thins before the stronger impression in the same way the telephone heaves because negation is built into each call besides loss is spelt in the absence of stars because we can hear sometimes what nothing is whenever we lose god in thought because we cannot think it free.

There are no ends but there are edges as if I dream of it but when it happens I forget how it happens or my pains are telling me apart but language creates world for as long as we believe in it so love stinks in the clothes but the sun rises in the skin although I feel depleted by each second but have nothing to add but time likewise a sentence is a tautology but in distant countries they may sing like love furthermore I walk back from the library with the rain on my skin but it is time to eat quickly the chocolate I bought so long before and we hold our heads under the sky but sometimes we dream we can see despite this the sun peels away another picture the same as the last but all the air says is wrong unless in the land of echoes we expect to hear a cloud come apart but gathering like deer in this forest are the few good

possible poems when we are constructing great answers but our faces
in the wind are torn after this waterfall is reversed but the road is
compiled from old lists similarly a stream spools under the bridge but
it stores birdcall and sunlight and will return it to the sea in contrast
the computer that knows my secret names is bleeding light but the
pieces of night feel apart consequently at the fragmentation factory
belts convey dust for the wind to deliver but time crashes into surfaces
and produces images that connect nightly further a figure is running
though my chambers but the smoke is very particular moreover
language evokes cancers in the brainstem but this is a song for the
wrong words or else the mouth hinges like a swingbinlid but the
apple walks away under its own laugh therefore a chance intelligence
arises out of the ether but conscious in its pure thought of the stars
ramifying against its certainty yet a language could have 'a various
and modulated grammatical system but only one word where the
clouds are in administration but the words fly on like bees to find
new senses on occasion the trees construct their answer but there
will be no one to hear as if language is describing why it should go
on but the more it talks the fewer answers it has since I walk to work
expecting to arrive but as I time the waves to sleep who is left to pray
but language hence I stretch my sands towards you but in the empty
hallways at the back of the head a new tenant is moving' similarly I
invest in the wrong books but poetry reads like an excuse the world
has for hanging around like this at times when ligatures connect my
speeches but I feel the enormous sun swallow my roof or your hands
idle across me but dust snakes the floor at times time travels through
me but the armies of light float in the hills nor is Father still waving
at the car that contained his parents but when they come back their
clothes are wrong in order that the moon plays those old 45s but we
do not dance in the lost versions of pastoral as if the news is the least
satisfactory part of a consumer's routine but it reflects the interests
of capital by evoking the right fears in the same way clouds explain
themselves in terms of what they leave behind but the sun no longer
applies itself while language's limbs member across matter but they
can't sing the shapes back to sleep when the cat stretches like a night
but I empty self of content unless time takes me by the hand but
surfaces quickly come to conclusions on the other hand the sun sets

inside but the dead are too busy helping us to see nor does each
road shatter its welds but cars maintain their evenings in the way that
from the quarry at the end of the mind come rocks the size of words
but the Concrete is still an abstraction because every word contains
a particle of enlightenment but they combine to make mud after
nothing answers but language but language can only answer as person.

tree : singing from the birds
truth : sleep through the moment of
world : disappear under the page
clouds : run out of steam
the sun : a point of view
thought : time's shadow
butterfly : winged hinge, hinged wing
Chomsky : this is the cheese the rat the cat caught stole
modernity : everything travelled faster but no one arrived
by walking : we connect with nothing
your money : where your mouth
I jotted much : my book is still empty
a swan at dusk : a flake of white under a coat of blue paint
what the things : the speaking stone the clock
speed dreaming : driving through mazes
the state reasons : state your reasons
when they arrive : the stars fit their destinations
stars, god's semen : all but one to die without fertilizing a thing
in a glass kingdom : light consists of water
too small to matter : for that reason infinite
in a chain of breaths : each link further from what is in the bucket
go deep says the eagle : rise high says the mole
the tides inside the eye : think about the stain in sustaining
under a mighty sentence : enough to let the words excite the surface
in the skin the sun sets in : red clouds harden into flower
the children eat your time : the sky will not outlast the day
collapsed cloud in the river : its depth
the stones are what we think : not the sand
there is a land inside this one : sometimes you can hear it reflecting
men run before their situation : sunlight guns them down
the car in my hands dissolves : the fire is in the water

a thick world curls about a leaf : there are rivers to unwind
entering the age of recurrences : we enter the age of recurrences
there are no visionary moments : outside time are no moments.
the animals make honest sounds : when you are gone they lie
a stream blubs over the one rock : perfects the sound to destroy it
beyond actually existing language : a poetry we're too weak to read
the faulty monsters are in motion : they are words
the clouds are tangled in the trees : are we thoughts that dissipate
a sense names the bird in its body : to see what a person is made of
the people we love pass into fiction : each poem an advert for decay
thoughts are too fragile for sentences : put them in soil
to write a long poem will be your task : water imagery predominates
people are not responsible for their cries : we speak to slice silence
your shadow on the stairs steps from you : scribbles report on water
language's limbs membering across matter : to sing world to sleep
when the trees have constructed an answer : there'll be none to hear
a group of words gangs up to form a sentence : the broken pasts
children cry from their rooms how they loved me : I cannot sleep

A page contains one as a bucket holds sunlight

the best are interesting misunderstandings

one is muddying the waters for a few moments longer

some are vehicles for connecting a thought to language

they form the kind of pattern historians dream about

or they are the best history we make for the robots

they are words put on a string

a person can leave their skin through one

some are machines made of language

sequences of statements provable or not in laboratories of mind

others display violence towards language

they can be an apparatus for putting thoughts in the wrong order

are when the depth of a thought is right for the length of the lines

one could be a fragment from an unfinishable sentence

many are the approach of thought to its possible perfection

the language arguing with itself and coming to no sound conclusion

once it was a raid on the articulate

they have stuff that is interested in the cracks in language

your eyes chase them but they go on as if language depended on it.

your shadows touch
you is broken
words curl around us
we pale before evenings
water is all shape
things remain to be said
things remain to be said
the stone sets in in the head
the roads are riding you
the map yawns
the dust will be returned
the airports are shut
sunrises are not repeated
stones think in the mouth
steam rises from cattle
space turns to stone
sleep is an afterthought
silence winds its world
rust is fire in slow motion
rivers speak in syllabic slur
rain is travelling
puddles collect their clouds
mouth is absence of thing
mist splits the second
midges form a thought
leaves are what are left
language speaks for yourself
clouds come to meet you
birdsongs seep from holes
birds walk a fine line
an object speaks for itself

all your jokes come true
air materializes
a tree leaks shadows
a field bears a track
a book stays open

shadows
broken
words
pale
water
things
remain
stone
roads
map
will
shut
not
think
from
space
sleep
winds
rust
slur
is
their
thing
the
form
left
speaks
to
seep
fine
itself

come
air
a
field
stays

Advertising, prodigal offspring of poetry.
Autobiography, unfinished suicide note.
Birds, severed hands.
Blood, ghost sitting inside you.
Body, skin stuffed with ghost.
Child, result of attrition between mass and time.
Definition, tautology.
Earth, a supper of bones.
Egg, moon's distant sister.
Eye, sucker of sense from sentences.
Façade, a fade in the face.
Fire, thought of matter.
Fist, empty hand.
Floor, grey sea lapping under the chairs.
Fruit, result of inaction.
Geese, future flutes of water.
Grass, complex sentence under the foot.
Head, language's limb.
History, passing expression on a landscape.
Humanity, dividing cells of future deity.
Infant, recording apparatus.
Life, dream of the inanimate.
Lives, parentheses in the same sentence.
Love, king of everywhere else.
Lovingly, as the dead wound the living.
Mind, medium for causation.
Mirror, persister of silence.
Mist, an accumulation of nothing.
Moth, winged hinge.
Mouth, a factory gate.
Night, shadow rotating across the planet.
Nothing, thing we don't see.
Now, the word for something else.
Nut, complicated space inside the tree.
Person, that which makes afraid the animals.
Poem, complex joy that the media dislikes.
Poetry, rain of sentences none of which are for the animals.

Self, a thought experiment.
Sister, distant cousin of the eye.
Sky, connecting tissue of cloud.
Smoke, capital of the nineteenth century.
Song, the lump in the throat.
Tautology, definition.
Thing, fragment of world.
Time, the secretary of the moon.
Tongue, stuck key.
Tree, stand for itself.
Word, dimly lit cathedral.
World, that which cannot be thought.
Wound, hole in the mind.

Advertising, theory of,	9
Autobiography, notes towards,	11
Birds, screams of,	12
Body, language of,	18
Child, dream of,	20
Definition, sketch toward,	25
Dream, see between,	27
Earth, insubstantiality of,	28
Egg, listening attitude,	31
Eye, fevered portion inside, is,	34
Fire, as an instrument of thought,	36
Floor, best or worst friend of the foot,	37
Fruit, its fight against silence,	38
Geese, swanness of,	40
God, see under,	41
Haiku, by god,	46
History, always too late,	49
Humanity, conceit of,	50
Idiot, joy of,	52
Infant, tragedy of,	55
Joyce, disinterred,	56
Language, body of,	57
Life, passim,	60
Lives, see others,	64
Love, is,	65
Mirror, op. cit.,	67
Mouth, end of,	69
Night, see day,	71
Mist, hazy idea of,	73
Mine, the coal of your darkness,	74
Newspaper Army, its columns,	77
Nothing,	78
Now, see past,	81
Nut, meaning of,	83
Person, see other,	85
Poem, to seek for, in this book,	86
Poetry, explanation for,	89

Say, run out of things to,   90
Sea, body of,   91
Self, see other,   93
Sky, see through,   95
Smoke, see over,   96
Song, words to,   97
Stone, songs for,   100
Tense, past,   102
Thing, thingness of,   103
Think, in itself,   105
Time, see over,   107
Tongue, feel,   109
Tree, inner workings,   110
Zukofsky, alluded to,   111

www.ingramcontent.com/pod-product-compliance
Lightning Source LLC
Chambersburg PA
CBHW031158160426
43193CB00008B/416